Sports Illustrated Kids: Legend vs. Legend

TOM BRADY

VS.

PEYTON MANNING

FOOTBALL LEGENDS FACE OFF

by Dionna L. Mann

CAPSTONE PRESS
a capstone imprint

Published by Capstone Press, an imprint of Capstone
1710 Roe Crest Drive, North Mankato, Minnesota 56003
capstonepub.com

Copyright © 2025 by Capstone. All rights reserved. No part of this publication may be reproduced in whole or in part, or stored in a retrieval system, or transmitted in any form or by any means, electronic, mechanical, photocopying, recording, or otherwise, without written permission of the publisher.

SPORTS ILLUSTRATED KIDS is a trademark of ABG-SI LLC.
Used with permission.

Library of Congress Cataloging-in-Publication Data is available
on the Library of Congress website.

ISBN: 9781669079866 (hardcover)
ISBN: 9781669079811 (paperback)
ISBN: 9781669079828 (ebook PDF)

Summary: Tom Brady and Peyton Manning are football superstars! Between the two, Brady has more career passing yards, but Manning leads in average passing yards per game. So which one is the all-time best? Young readers can decide for themselves by comparing the fantastic feats and stunning stats of two legendary
pro football players.

Editorial Credits
Editor: Christopher Harbo; Designer: Sarah Bennett; Media Researcher: Svetlana Zhurkin; Production Specialist: Katy LaVigne

Image Credits
Associated Press: Kevin Rivoli, 12, Paul Spinelli, 16, Tom DiPace, 11; Getty Images: Adam Glanzman, 25, Al Bello, cover (left), Andy Lyons, cover (right), Bob Levey, 27, Brian Bahr, 26, Doug Pensinger, 5, 15, 17, Dustin Bradford, 6, Elsa, 20, Ezra Shaw, 21, 22, 28, Gregory Shamus, 19, Jim McIsaac, 14, Joe Robbins, 8, Justin Edmonds, 10, Michael B. Thomas, 24, Mike Carlson, 7, Patrick Smith, 23, Win McNamee, 18; Newscom: UPI Photo Service/Bruce Gordon, 13; Shutterstock: saicle (background), cover and throughout; Sports Illustrated: Erick W. Rasco, 4, 9, 29

Any additional websites and resources referenced in this book are not maintained, authorized, or sponsored by Capstone. All product and company names are trademarks™ or registered® trademarks of their respective holders.

CONTENTS

Quarterback Legends Face Off! **4**

Passing Yards **6**

Passing Completions **8**

Strong Arm 400+ **10**

Rushing Yards **12**

Pass, Catch, Score **14**

Long Yardage Touchdowns **16**

Tuck, Run, and Score **18**

For the Win **20**

Super Bowl Champs **22**

Pro Bowls and All Pros **24**

Most Valuable Player **26**

Face Off Winner? **28**

Glossary **30**

Read More **31**

Internet Sites **31**

Index **32**

About the Author **32**

Words in **bold** appear in the glossary.

Quarterback Legends Face Off!

Tom Brady and Peyton Manning were great NFL quarterbacks. They cut through **defenses**. They scored **touchdowns**. They even played in 14 Super Bowls combined! But which one was the greatest quarterback of all time? Stack their stats side-by-side to decide!

Tom Brady

Peyton Manning

THE MATCHUP	Born	State
Brady	August 3, 1977	California
Manning	March 24, 1976	Louisiana

Passing Yards

Brady and Manning were passing superstars. Their passes soared downfield. During his **career**, Manning passed for 71,940 total **yards**. That is an **average** of 270.5 yards per game. Brady threw for 89,214 yards. He averaged 266.3 yards per game.

Manning drops back to pass.

Brady slings the football downfield.

THE MATCHUP	Career Passing Yards	Average Passing Yards Per Game
Manning	71,940	270.5
Brady	89,214	266.3

Passing Completions

Brady and Manning both worked magic with their **receivers**. Their throws almost always hit their targets. In his career, Manning completed 6,125 passes. That's an average of 23.0 passes per game. Brady completed 7,753 passes. He averaged 23.1 per game.

Manning looks for a receiver while playing against the Indianapolis Colts.

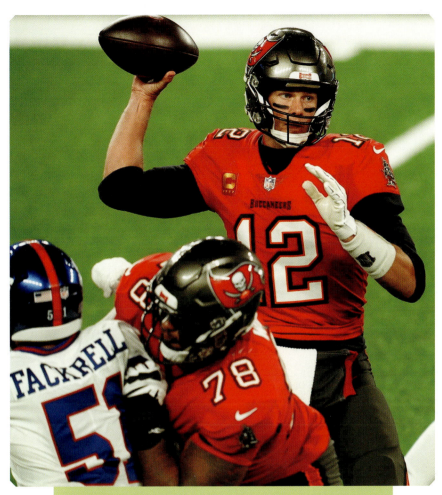

Brady gets ready to pass in a game against the New York Giants.

THE MATCHUP	Passing Completions	Average Completions Per Game
Manning	6,125	23.0
Brady	7,753	23.1

Strong Arm 400+

Passing 400 yards or more in a single game is rare. But both Brady and Manning did it 14 times! Manning's best game was on October 5, 2014. He passed for 479 yards. Brady's best game was on September 12, 2011. He passed for a whopping 517 yards!

Manning launches a pass over the Arizona Cardinals' defense.

Brady hurls a powerful pass during the game in which he reached his best passing yards.

THE MATCHUP	400+ Passing Yards in a Game	Most Passing Yards in a Game
Manning	14	479
Brady	14	517

Rushing Yards

Quarterbacks don't always pass the ball. Sometimes they run with it! During his career, Manning **rushed** for 667 yards. Brady rushed for 1,123 yards. But Manning's regular season best tops Brady's. In 2001, Manning rushed for 157 yards. Brady topped out at 110 yards in 2002.

Manning runs 33 yards for a touchdown in a 2001 game.

Brady escapes the St. Louis Rams' defense while rushing.

THE MATCHUP	Career Rushing Yards	Season Best Rushing Yards
Manning	667	157
Brady	1,123	110

Pass, Catch, Score

Both Brady and Manning had a ton of passing touchdowns. Brady is the all-time leader with 649. Manning trails him with 539. But Manning has the most passing touchdowns in a season. He had 55. Brady's season best was 50.

Brady passes for a touchdown against the Miami Dolphins.

Manning flings a touchdown pass for the Denver Broncos.

THE MATCHUP	Career Passing Touchdowns	Season High Passing Touchdowns
Brady	649	50
Manning	539	55

15

Long Yardage Touchdowns

Long yardage touchdowns make fans leap from their seats. Both Brady and Manning have some doozies. In 2011, Brady passed to Wes Welker who jetted 99 yards for a touchdown. In 2014, Manning connected with Demaryius Thomas who zipped in an 86-yard touchdown.

Wes Welker runs 99 yards for a touchdown.

Demaryius Thomas sprints for an 86-yard touchdown.

THE MATCHUP	Longest Touchdown	Receiver
Brady	99 yards	Wes Welker
Manning	86 yards	Demaryius Thomas

17

Tuck, Run, and Score

Brady and Manning were pros at connecting with their receivers. But sometimes they scored all by themselves. During his career, Brady had 28 rushing touchdowns. Manning had 18. Both quarterbacks had 4 rushing touchdowns in a single season. Brady did it in 2012. Manning did it in 2001 and 2006.

Brady celebrates a touchdown during a Super Bowl.

Manning scores a touchdown against the Miami Dolphins.

THE MATCHUP	Career Rushing Touchdowns	Season High Rushing Touchdowns
Brady	28	4
Manning	18	4

19

For the Win

Starting quarterbacks play to win. In 23 seasons, Brady started and won 251 regular season games. He also won 35 **playoff** games. In 17 seasons, Manning started and won 186 regular season games. He won 14 playoff games.

Photographers swarm around Brady after the New England Patriots won the 2015 AFC Championship game.

Manning waves to the crowd after defeating Tom Brady and the New England Patriots in the 2016 AFC Championship game.

THE MATCHUP	Regular Season Wins	Playoff Wins
Brady	251	35
Manning	186	14

Super Bowl Champs

Both Brady and Manning are Super Bowl champs. Manning played in four Super Bowls. He won two in 2007 and 2016. Brady played in 10 Super Bowls. He won seven of them! He was unbeatable in 2002, 2004, 2005, 2015, 2017, 2019, and 2021!

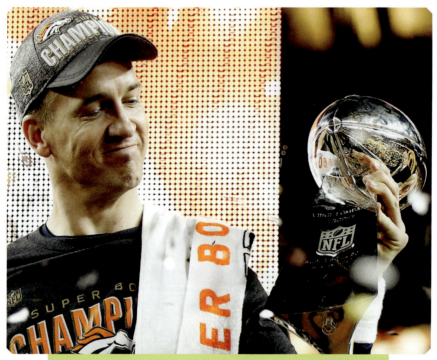

Manning holds the 2016 Super Bowl trophy.

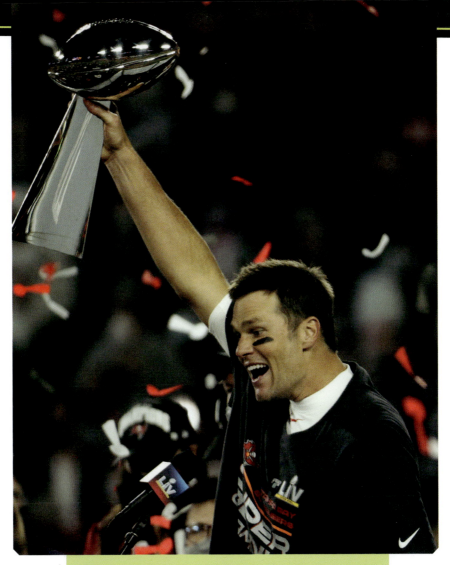

Brady raises the 2021 Super Bowl trophy after his team's win.

THE MATCHUP	Super Bowls Played	Super Bowls Won
Manning	4	2
Brady	10	7

Pro Bowls and All Pros

Only the best NFL players earn Pro Bowl and All-Pro honors. Manning made 14 Pro Bowls. Brady made 15! Brady was chosen for the All-Pro First Team three times. Manning was selected seven times!

Manning passing for the Denver Broncos

Brady rushing for the New England Patriots

THE MATCHUP	Pro Bowl Appearances	All-Pro First Team Selections
Manning	14	7
Brady	15	3

Most Valuable Player

Being named an **MVP** is a high honor. In the NFL, players can be named **league** MVP and Super Bowl MVP. Manning was named league MVP five times. He was the Super Bowl MVP once. Brady was chosen as league MVP three times. He was the Super Bowl MVP five times!

Manning was named the Super Bowl MVP in 2007.

Brady with his Super Bowl MVP award in 2017

THE MATCHUP	NFL MVP Awards	Super Bowl MVP Awards
Manning	5	1
Brady	3	5

Face Off Winner?

Manning and Brady will go down in history as great NFL quarterbacks. They both threw perfect passes. They both rushed for touchdowns. And they both won multiple Super Bowls.

Who do you think was the greatest quarterback of all time? You make the call!

Peyton Manning

Tom Brady

Glossary

average (AV-uh-rij)—a number found by adding a group of figures together and then dividing the sum by the number of figures that were added

career (kuh-REER)—a person's main work over a large part of their life

defense (DEE-fens)—the team that tries to stop points from being scored; the defense is the team that doesn't have the ball

league (LEEG)—a group of sports teams that play against each other

MVP (EM-VEE-PEE)—short for most valuable player

playoff (PLAY-awf)—a series of games played after the regular season to decide a championship

receiver (ri-SEE-vur)—a football player who catches passes from a quarterback

rush (RUHSH)—when an offensive player behind the line of scrimmage runs with the football

touchdown (TUCH-down)—a play in football in which a team carries the ball into the opponent's end zone for six points

yard (YARD)—a unit of measurement equal to three feet

Read More

Buckley, James Jr. *Who Is Tom Brady?* New York: Penguin Workshop, 2021.

Greenberg, Keith Elliot. *Patrick Mahomes vs. Peyton Manning: Who Would Win?* Minneapolis: Lerner Publishing Group, 2024.

Tustison, Matt. *Super NFL Quarterbacks.* Mankato, MN: Black Rabbit Books, 2025.

Internet Sites

Britannica Kids: Peyton Manning
kids.britannica.com/students/article/Peyton-Manning/544863

Britannica Kids: Tom Brady
kids.britannica.com/students/article/Tom-Brady/623636

Kiddle: American Football Facts for Kids
kids.kiddle.co/American_football

Index

awards
    All-Pro honors, 24–25
    MVPs, 26–27

birthdays, 5
birthplaces, 5

passing completions, 8–9
passing yards, 6–7, 10–11
Pro Bowls, 24–25

rushing yards, 12–13

Super Bowls, 4, 22–23, 26–27, 28

touchdowns
    long yardage, 16–17
    passing, 14–15
    rushing, 18–19, 28

wins
    playoff, 20–21
    regular season, 20–21

About the Author

Photo by Dionna L. Mann

Dionna L. Mann is a children's book author and freelance journalist. She spent more than 25 years volunteering and working in the school system where her talented children attended. Dionna's favorite part of working with children was teaching them about writing and reading their heartfelt words. As a person of color, she enjoys learning about lesser-known people found in the records of African American history. You can find Dionna online at dionnalmann.com.